THIS LAND CALLED AMERICA: **MONTANA**

CREATIVE EDUCATION

Published by Creative Education
P.O. Box 227, Mankato, Minnesota 56002
Creative Education is an imprint of The Creative Company
www.thecreativecompany.us

Design by Blue Design (www.bluedes.com)
Art direction by Rita Marshall
Book production by The Design Lab
Printed in the United States of America

Photographs by Alamy (Richard Cummins, E.R. Degginger, Montana Stock
Photography, Photo Art Collection, Visions of America, LLC), Corbis (Bett-
mann, Frank Lane Picture Agency, JOHN GRESS/Reuters, Andrew Holbrooke,
Joel W. Rogers, Shepard Sherbell, Stapleton Collection, Jim Sugar), Dream-
stime (Fjs, Granitepeaker), Getty Images (FPG, Kate Thompson), iStockphoto
(Steve Byland, Christian Sawicki)

Library of Congress Cataloging-in-Publication Data
Peterson, Sheryl.
Montana / by Sheryl Peterson.
p. cm. — (This land called America)
Includes bibliographical references and index.
ISBN 978-1-58341-779-9
1. Montana—Juvenile literature. I. Title. II. Series.
F731.3.P48 2009
978.6—dc22   2008009508

First Edition
9 8 7 6 5 4 3 2 1

This Land Called America

MONTANA

SHERYL PETERSON

Montana

SHERYL PETERSON

SNOWCAPPED MOUNTAINS RISE UP OVERHEAD. WILD ROSES BLOOM NEAR THE PATH. VISITORS TO MONTANA SET OFF ON A DAYLONG HIKING ADVENTURE. THEY LACE UP THEIR BOOTS AND SLIP ON THEIR BACKPACKS. THE HIKERS PACK EXTRA WATER, TRAIL MAPS, AND SUNSCREEN. ON THEIR WALK, THE ADVENTURERS SPY WHITE-TAILED DEER AND ELK. THEY CATCH A GLIMPSE OF MOUNTAIN GOATS AND A GIANT MOOSE. TINY SPARROWS CHIRP, AND EAGLES SOAR OVERHEAD. THE HIKERS REST AND DIP THEIR FEET IN A CHILLY STREAM. HANDFULS OF SWEET HUCKLEBERRIES PROVIDE INSTANT ENERGY. THE FRESH AIR IS GREAT, BUT WHAT THE HIKERS LOVE MOST IS THE AMAZING MONTANA SCENERY.

YEAR

1743 French brothers François and Louis de La Vérendrye explore southeastern Montana.

EVENT

Last of the Wilderness

THE CROW AND CHEYENNE INDIANS WERE THE EARLIEST INHABITANTS OF MONTANA. THEY LIVED ON THE VAST GRASSLANDS AND RUGGED MOUNTAINS. THE INDIANS HUNTED BIG HERDS OF BUFFALO AND COOKED THE MEAT OVER THEIR CAMPFIRES. THEY CARVED BUFFALO BONES INTO NEEDLES FOR SEWING BUFFALO HIDES INTO

clothing. The Indians fished in the clear streams and gathered roots and berries in the forests.

In 1743, French brothers François and Louis de La Vérendrye explored the southeastern corner of Montana while looking for furbearing animals. They saw what they described as "shining mountains" in the distance. These were most likely Montana's Bighorn Mountains.

Years later, in 1803, France sold a huge area of land called the Louisiana Territory to the United States. It included Montana. President Thomas Jefferson sent Meriwether Lewis and William Clark to explore the unknown land. The men and their guides left St. Louis and canoed up the Missouri River into Montana.

As Sacagawea led Lewis and Clark (above) through Montana in 1805, they encountered many groups of American Indians (opposite).

YEAR
1805
EVENT

Meriwether Lewis and William Clark reach Montana by way of North Dakota and the Missouri River.

By 1870, six years after gold was discovered there, Helena had become a major city in the territory.

Helena, Montana

Lewis and Clark carefully recorded their observations in journals. The men drew maps of mountains, waterfalls, and rivers. They sketched pine trees and elk. Lewis and Clark returned to St. Louis and boasted about Montana's wild beauty and many furbearing animals.

Soon, American and British fur companies began to arrive in Montana. In 1829, John Jacob Astor established the American Fur Company and several fur-trading forts in northern Montana. Steamboats began to puff their way up the Missouri River to reach Fort Benton. Today, the small town is known as the "Birthplace of Montana."

In the mid-1800s, however, the fur trade dwindled. Animals that were hunted for their fur, such as beavers, became scarce. Buffalo hides became popular to use for clothing and saddles. Hunters killed millions of buffalo, taking the hides and leaving the bodies to rot on the prairie.

In 1862, gold fever hit Montana. Prospectors bragged of big nuggets being found in Grasshopper Creek in the southwestern corner of the state. Soon, Helena, Bannack, and Virginia City popped up as mining boomtowns. Bozeman and Missoula prospered as mining supply centers. Two years after the discovery of gold, Montana was made a U.S. territory.

When the gold fever died down, many people became ranchers. The era of the long cattle drives began. From 1866

YEAR
1862 Gold is first discovered in Grasshopper Creek in southwestern Montana near Bannack.
EVENT

until 1887, cowboys herded cattle from Texas north to Montana. Cattle grazed on Montana's lush grasslands and were then sold to markets in the East.

From the 1850s through the 1870s, many people moved into Montana and pushed the Indians off their hunting grounds. The Indians fought back. On June 25, 1876, General George Custer led a small army of about 300 soldiers toward a large Indian village near the Little Bighorn River in southeastern Montana. Custer and his men were outnumbered and killed by Sioux and Cheyenne Indians led by Chief Sitting Bull. The battle was known as "Custer's Last Stand." Later, more soldiers arrived and forced the Indians to surrender. The Indians moved onto government lands called reservations.

Montana settled into peaceful times at the end of the 1800s. Farming became prosperous, and three railroad lines soon crossed the territory. On November 8, 1889, President Benjamin Harrison proclaimed Montana to be America's 41st state. Joseph K. Toole of Helena served as the first governor. Within its first 30 years of statehood, Montana's population nearly quadrupled, reaching 548,889 by 1920.

After serving in the Civil War, General George Custer (opposite, seated) continued his army career by fighting Indians until his death at the Little Bighorn (above).

YEAR

1876   The Sioux and Cheyenne defeat General George Custer's troops in "Custer's Last Stand."

EVENT

- 10 -

Land of Shining Mountains

This Land Called AMERICA

THE STATE OF MONTANA IS ALMOST RECTANGULAR IN SHAPE. MONTANA IS BORDERED TO THE NORTH BY THE CANADIAN PROVINCES OF BRITISH COLUMBIA, SASKATCHEWAN, AND ALBERTA. THE STATES OF NORTH DAKOTA AND SOUTH DAKOTA LIE TO THE EAST. IDAHO AND WYOMING FORM THE STATE'S WESTERN AND SOUTHERN BORDERS.

Montana is fourth in size after Alaska, Texas, and California. However, the state is ranked 44th in population. That means that people in Montana have lots of room. The Great Plains area of eastern Montana is a sea of waving grasses and small mountain ranges. Colorful wildflowers such as lupine, shooting stars, and Indian paintbrush are scattered across the prairie. Everywhere there is a perfect view of the clear blue sky. That's why Montana is called "Big Sky Country."

Western Montana has rugged hills and mountains with snowcapped peaks. The state's highest point is Granite Peak in the south-central Beartooth Range. Granite Peak is 12,799 feet (3,901 m) tall. Elers Koch, a Montana forester, was the first man to successfully make it to the top of Granite Peak in 1923. Today, many people spend one day climbing until they reach "Froze-to-Death Plateau." After camping there overnight, they scale the icy rocks to the top.

Tall cottonwoods and stout red cedars grow in Montana's forests, along with grand ponderosa pines, the state tree. Montana ranks as one of the top states in the country for viewing wildlife. Visitors can see bighorn sheep and grizzly bears in the mountain areas. Prairie dogs, martens, pronghorn, and hoary marmots live on the flat, grassy plains.

Mountains such as Granite Peak (opposite) break up the flat landscape that shows off Montana's famously big skies (above).

YEAR
1881 The Utah and Northern Pacific Railroad enters Montana, connecting Salt Lake City, Utah, to Butte.
EVENT

- 13 -

T he Continental Divide zigzags along the top of the Rockies, which local Indians call the "backbone of the world." The Divide is an invisible line that marks the direction in which water flows. Rivers on the eastern side of the line flow to the Atlantic Ocean. Rivers on the western side flow to the Pacific Ocean.

In 1894, people began noticing small blue pebbles in the streams near Yogo Gulch in central Montana. Yogo Gulch had been a gold rush boomtown for years, but then people realized that the stones were valuable gemstones called sapphires. Yogo Gulch mines became famous for their clear, cornflower-blue sapphires. Other mines in the state produced silver, iron ore, and lead.

Logan Pass in Glacier National Park (opposite) is a good starting point for a hike along the Continental Divide, while those interested in sapphires can watch miners at work (above).

1910

The U.S. Congress creates Glacier National Park, located in northwestern Montana.

The 300-foot-deep
(91 m) Flathead Lake
receives its water
from the Flathead
and Swan rivers.

Northern Montana's Flathead Lake is the largest freshwater lake west of the Mississippi River. It is famous for deep-water fishing and the cherry orchards on its eastern shore. Flathead Lake also has an island that was once home to wild horses. Today, the island provides a safe place for bighorn sheep and bald eagles to live.

The weather in Montana is milder and drier than most people expect. Western Montana has warmer winters and cooler summers than the eastern plains. The average overall state temperature varies from 28 °F (-2 °C) in January to 84 °F (29 °C) in July.

The mild weather gives adventuresome Montanans the chance to enjoy the outdoors year-round. Many people go boating on the state's two largest waterways—the Yellowstone and Missouri rivers. According to the Guinness World Records, Montana also lays claim to the shortest river in the world. The Roe River flows for 200 feet (61 m) between Giant Springs and the Missouri River near Great Falls in western Montana.

Montana mountains such as Granite Peak provide a good habitat in which mountain goats can thrive.

YEAR
1914   Montana women receive the right to vote.
EVENT

Hearty Montanans

THE FACE OF MONTANA HAS CHANGED A LOT OVER
THE YEARS. FUR TRADERS AND GOLD PROSPECTORS
CAME AND LEFT IN THE 19TH CENTURY. NATIVE INDIAN
TRIBES WERE MOVED ONTO RESERVATIONS IN NORTHERN
AND EASTERN PARTS OF THE STATE. RICH, WIDE-OPEN
PRAIRIE LAND MADE MONTANA ATTRACTIVE TO
PIONEERS INTERESTED IN FARMING.

In the early 1900s, Americans traveled west to Montana
from the eastern U.S. Immigrants arrived from Germany,
Canada, Norway, and England. Some of Montana's immigrant
groups have remained close-knit. The Hutterites, a religious
group of German descent, live together on the central prairie
in groups called colonies. They make their own clothes and
live simply. The colonies produce most of Montana's supply
of pork and eggs. The mining town of Red Lodge has many
diverse nationalities. Every August, the city hosts a Festival
of Nations to honor everyone's heritage.

Montana was a good place for building ranches (opposite) and raising children in safe communities, as the Hutterites (above) did.

YEAR

1916   Jeannette Rankin becomes the first woman elected to the U.S. House of Representatives.

EVENT

Great Falls, Montana's third-largest city at just over 58,000 people, features a grand courthouse built in 1903.

Today, more than half of all Montanans live in small cities. Billings, Great Falls, and Missoula are the only cities with a population greater than 55,000 people. About 90 percent of Montanans today are white. American Indians make up six percent of the population of Montana. Recently, people have moved to the state from Laos and Mexico as well.

Many people in Montana continue to farm or raise cattle. Montana has some of the nation's largest sheep and cattle ranches. People raise wheat, barley, sugar beets, and potatoes. Besides farming, many people work in the petroleum and natural gas industries. Others have jobs in transportation. Because of Montana's vast distances, taking care of the highways and railroads is important. Montana is a long state. Most roads in Montana run from the east to the west. There are very few north-south highways.

YEAR

1943 In July, Fort Peck Dam on the Missouri River begins generating electricity in northeastern Montana.

EVENT

Although the city of Billings is the largest in the state, the surrounding area is used for farmland.

CHAS. M. RUSSELL

COPYRIGHT 1902 BY CHARLES GIES, GREAT FALLS, MONT.

"THE COWBOY ARTIST."

Thousands of Montanans are employed in the tourism business. They work at Montana's 50 state parks, 2 national parks, and numerous ski areas. Whatever they do for work, though, Montanans love to play in the great outdoors of their western state. Some ski and hike in the mountains. Others fish and go boating on Montana's rivers and lakes. Many people golf, ride horses, or compete in rodeos.

One Montanan with a passion for outdoor adventure was painter Charles M. Russell. Russell came to the state in 1880, when he was 16. He lived as a trapper and a cowboy. Later in life, Russell became one of the most famous painters of the Old West. He painted cowboys, Indians, galloping horses, and the beautiful Montana landscape.

Works by artist Charles M. Russell can be seen at the C. M. Russell Museum in Great Falls.

Whitefish Mountain Resort, established in 1947 near Flathead Lake, attracts adventurous winter skiers.

YEAR

1959 Severe earthquakes of a 7.5 magnitude hit the Hebgen Lake area in southwestern Montana.

EVENT

Robert "Evel" Knievel was another colorful Montanan. Knievel was born in Butte and became a motorcycle trick rider in the early 1960s. He jumped through rings of fire. Once, he leaped over 14 buses. He is most famous for attempting to fly over a portion of Idaho's Snake River Canyon. When Knievel's parachute opened too early, it ended his risky feat, but it saved his life.

Montanans value education, and Jeannette Rankin was an early supporter of education for all. Rankin was born in Missoula and attended the University of Montana. She campaigned for women's suffrage, or the right to vote. In 1916, Rankin became the first woman in America to be elected to the U.S. Congress. In 1968, at age 87, Rankin led a peace march in Washington, D.C., to protest the Vietnam War.

Evel Knievel regularly attempted dangerous feats in vehicles such as the "Sky-Cycle" (above), but Jeannette Rankin (opposite) opposed all forms of violence.

Raging forest fires in Yellowstone National Park burn more than 36 percent of the park.

Heart of the West

This Land Called AMERICA

MILLIONS OF YEARS AGO, MONTANA WAS HOME TO SOME GIGANTIC CREATURES. TODAY, PEOPLE INTERESTED IN DINOSAURS CAN FOLLOW "THE DINOSAUR TRAIL" THROUGHOUT EASTERN AND CENTRAL MONTANA. THE 15 POINTS OF INTEREST ALONG THE TRAIL GIVE PEOPLE PLENTY OF OPPORTUNITIES TO INVESTIGATE MUSEUMS AND SEE WORKING FOSSIL FIELDS.

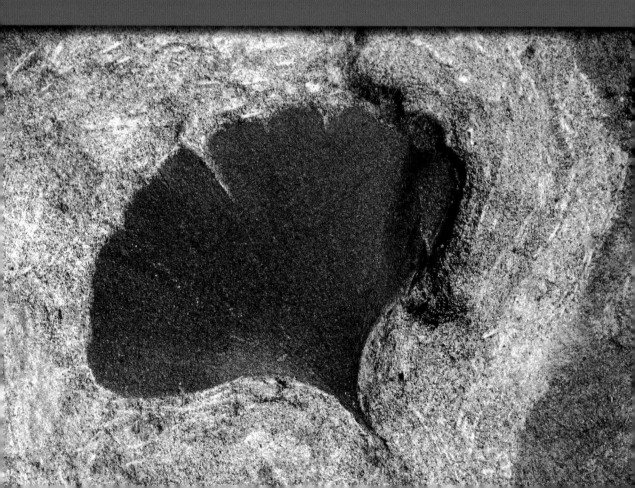

In fossil fields, scientists called paleontologists dig up the earth. They preserve the fossils, or the remains, of ancient animals and plants. Inside the Fort Peck Interpretive Center in northeastern Montana is "Peck's Rex," a life-size skeleton of a 15-foot-tall (4.5 m) tyrannosaurus rex. At the Carver County Museum in southeastern Montana, visitors marvel at several complete triceratops skulls.

Visitors to Montana don't want to miss Montana's famous natural treasures—Yellowstone National Park and Glacier National Park. Yellowstone was established as America's first national park in 1872. The park is located in southwestern Montana and parts of Wyoming and Idaho. Grizzly bears, buffalo, elk, and wolves roam the park. People also come to see the spouting hot springs. The most famous geyser is called Old Faithful. It shoots up a spray of steamy water about every 94 minutes.

Natural effects such as the warm water of hot springs (above) and the fossils of plants (opposite) and dinosaurs draw visitors to the state.

Glacier National Park, in northern Montana, is a wilderness area of more than 1 million acres (404,686 ha). The park has more than 700 miles (1,127 km) of hiking trails. Visitors tromp

YEAR
1996   On April 3, the FBI captures American terrorist Theodore Kaczynski, the "Unabomber," near Lincoln, Montana.
EVENT

- 27 -

through mountain meadows dotted with flowers such as queen's cup and rock clematis. They backpack through rocky terrain to find clear glacial lakes in which they can fish for trout and salmon. Lake McDonald is the largest lake in the park. It was carved out by an ancient glacier and is 10 miles (16 km) long.

Tourists driving along Interstate 90 in south-central Montana often take a side trip to Greycliff Prairie Dog Town State Park. People grab their cameras and watch the blacktailed prairie dogs pop up and down out of their underground homes. Visitors to the park can picnic while the curious, playful animals entertain them.

Although Montana has no professional sports teams, Montanans love their college sports. There is an ongoing rivalry between the University of Montana Grizzlies in Missoula and the Montana State Bobcats in Bozeman. Both colleges have successful football, basketball, and soccer teams, along with many other sports.

Baseball has been popular in Montana since the mining camp days of the 1860s. The Missoula Osprey and the Billings Mustangs are two minor-league teams that play in the Pioneer League. Dave McNally, a Billings native, pitched for the major-league Baltimore Orioles in the 1960s and '70s.

The University of Montana men's basketball program had won six Big Sky Conference titles as of 2009.

YEAR

2000 Wildfires scorch thousands of acres and burn more than 320 homes in the western Bitterroot Valley region.

EVENT

QUICK FACTS

Population: 957,861

Largest city: Billings (pop. 101,876)

Capital: Helena

Entered the union: November 8, 1889

Nicknames: Treasure State, Big Sky Country

State flower: bitterroot

State bird: western meadowlark

Size: 147,042 square miles (380,837 sq km)—4th-biggest in U.S.

Major industries: mining, ranching, tourism

Curiously, cows outnumber people three to one in Montana. The midwestern city of Detroit, Michigan, contains about the same number of people as are in the entire state of Montana. But Montanans love the space, fresh air, and clean water that their state provides.

Visitors to Montana can't wait to explore the state's prairies and mountains. They hike the state's trails, ski down the snowy mountains, and search for white-tailed deer. Montana is a land of rugged, western wonder that all kinds of people can enjoy. There is plenty of elbow room and spectacular scenery to spare for everyone who makes their home under the big skies of Montana.

BIBLIOGRAPHY

Box, C. J. *Travel Smart*. New York: Avalon Travel Publishing, 2000.

Gottberg, John. *Hidden Montana*. Berkeley, Calif.: Ulysses Press, 2005.

Montana State Tourism Office. "Lewis and Clark in Montana." State of Montana. http://visitmt.com/landc2.htm.

Schneider, Bill, and Russ Schneider. *Hiking Montana*. Helena, Mont.: Falcon Press, 2004.

Spencer, Janet. *Montana Trivia*. Helena, Mont.: Riverbend Publishing, 2005.

INDEX